Embracing STEM Smarts

An Encouraging Guide for Young Ladies Who Have a Passion for STEM

Alexis M. Scott

Embracing STEM Smarts: An Encouraging Guide for Young
Ladies Who Have a Passion for STEM

Embracing STEM Smarts: An Encouraging Guide for Young
Ladies Who Have a Passion for STEM

1. Education 2. General

ISBN-10: 1547180455

ISBN-13: 978-1547180455

Embracing STEM Smarts Authors

ALEXIS M. SCOTT

Why did I choose STEM?

This is a very good question. Before I answer, I need to provide a bit of background about me that will give credence to my response. My name is Alexis M. Scott. I have a Bachelor's of Science Degree and a Master's of Science Degree in Mathematics. I went to undergraduate school in Atlanta at Spelman College. I attended graduate School at the University of North Texas in Denton. My first career opportunity was as a data analyst at M.I.T Lincoln Laboratory and from there I held a variety of engineering positions at various defense organizations; working in California, Connecticut, DC Metro Area, internships in Pittsburgh and Georgia Tech. In addition to my engineering positions, I was also able to maintain a position as a part-time college professor of mathematics. I would work engineering during the day and teach mathematics to college students in the evenings and weekends. Wherever I worked as an engineer, I maintained a part-time position as a college professor. I consider myself a Triple-E: educator, entrepreneur, and engineer. These fields encompass who I am and are a result of how STEM has affected my life.

I call myself an educator because I have worked in my passion of mathematics education for over 25 years. I began tutoring at an early age. I always wanted people to understand what they were missing. When I started my undergraduate studies, I was completely in my element because I began working in the math lab. I received so much satisfaction from that opportunity that I also began tutoring others in my dorm. When I graduated, and attended graduate school,

I continued tutoring in the math lab. I also began teaching courses as an assistant to a professor. It was then that I fully realized what I was supposed to be doing. I understood one of my greatest gifts and a full-on passion for math education was born. My greatest gratification is seeing the lightbulb moment when a student finally gets it.

I founded AMS Academic Solutions to expound on my love of mathematics and academic education. I did not strive to be an entrepreneur. I wanted to be a tutor. I saw it as a way to make a few extra bucks. A hobby. However, as I tutored, I began noticing the challenges students were having with math and potentially other subjects. Students were having a lot of frustrations and I sought to alleviate those frustrations. There was a void that needed to be filled. From this void, a business venture was born.

I am an engineer because that was my beginning career that allowed me to follow my passion. I began my career as a data analyst at M.I.T Lincoln Laboratories. Data analysis transformed into computer programming. What I soon realized is after I mastered one computer language, it was very simple to understand other computer languages. I could take the data I analyzed and create programs to model this analysis still using my love of mathematics to develop these calculations. From computer programming and analyzing data, I made a final transition to a new field of engineering at the time called information assurance (you may know it now by the more common moniker of cyber security); which lead me to managing a team of engineers. Engineering is my angel investor. My engineering career has allowed me to follow my educator and entrepreneurial passions.

Let's return to the question. Did I choose any of these STEM fields? I can answer with a resounding No! Growing up, I wanted to be a photographer. I did not have a creative eye for taking pictures; I was just fascinated with the machinations of how a camera worked. After my photography phase ended, I decided I wanted to be an accountant; only because accountants get to count money. And I loved counting money. So that is where it started. I wanted to be an accountant and sit in an office all day and count money. Then fate intervened. The college that I chose (Spelman College) did not have an accounting major. I really wanted to attend that college above all else. I needed to align myself with a major that still would allow me being an accountant. Mathematics was the most obvious choice. I started down a path that would inevitably define who I am as an educator, an entrepreneur, and an engineer. To answer the initial question: Why did I choose STEM? I didn't. STEM chose me. I am so glad that it did! Once I embraced this STEM passion, I never looked back and have never regretted that decision.

Fear of the SMARTS

I am a smart woman. I always have been. Learning was extremely easy for me. But girls were not supposed to be smart. Especially smart in the subjects where I excelled which were math and the sciences. Girls were supposed to be cute and at times I felt that my intelligence was a liability. I can distinctly remember getting a 100 on a biology test in middle school and having to prove to my teacher that I didn't cheat by taking the test again. It was not appreciated that I had really studied and deserved that grade. But it was concluded incorrectly that the only way that I could have received a 100 was to have cheated. That event left an impression on me. I mistakenly deduced that I was not supposed to be smart, since my intelligence was going to be continually questioned at every turn. Because of this fear of being constantly challenged, I began to hide my intelligence. I would do just enough to get a good grade; but not too much to stand out. It was not until I reached high school before I really began to appreciate how smart I was. But part of me even then regretted the time I wasted in controlling my smarts. Too much wasted energy on that fear that could have been more appropriately used to strengthen me and help me to grow.

How can you overcome the fear of the smarts?

- You must be You!
  It took me far too long to embrace what I was and I always wanted to conform to what people were comfortable with. They were comfortable and I was miserable. I can honestly tell you, you will never be happy being anything other than yourself. If you are smart. Be Smart!

- Understand that there is nothing to fear. It is ok to be smart. As a young girl, I was afraid of how people would perceive me in being as intelligent as I was. But I had the incorrect perception. Fear immobilizes you. You cannot move forward, and you have gone too far to turn around and go back. Grasp that there is truly nothing to fear and tackle your STEM subject.

- Don't allow the fear to keep you from excelling. I stopped wanting to be smart, because I felt consistently challenged to prove how smart I was. Now step up to the challenge and defeat it so well, that you will not be challenged again. Grow fully into what you are and appreciate what you are supposed to be.

It is sometimes lonely being the only one.

I went to Spelman College from August 1989 – May 1993. If I had known that would be the last time where I was not the minority in a group, I would have appreciated it more. What do I mean by that statement? Well Spelman College is a woman's institution of higher learning. Specifically, women of African-American descent. Women from all over were excelling in the **S**ciences, **T**echnology, **E**ngineering and **M**athematics (STEM). It was encouraging; wonderful to both to see and experience. But little did I know that it was also an anomaly. Because after I graduated in May of 1993, little did I expect that I would never have an opportunity like that again; being a part of a huge group of African-American Women who excelled in the STEM fields.

When I entered graduate school, I was the only African-American female in that entering class for mathematics. Additionally, I was one of two women. It was a daunting experience. I was the mythical unicorn and I always felt with my male peers that I had to work twice as hard to prove that I deserved to be there. After I graduated in December of 1995, I went to work at MIT Lincoln Laboratory as an analyst. I was one of two African-Americans in my group and one of three women. But I was the only African-American woman. For my next 4 employers, I was one of a very disproportionate number of African-American females in my group. I currently manage a group of 13 engineers. I am the only African-American female manager in my department. STEM knowledge is universal. STEM experience however is not.

Early in my career, I felt that to be heard that I had to raise the level of my voice. It was very difficult to find someone that I could relate these feelings to that would completely understand my situation. If you are the majority, it is hard to explain to someone who is in the minority how to act in certain situations. It is a very isolating feeling but once I found someone to talk to who could also relate in the experience, I did not feel so alone. The feelings I was having was not unique to me and that others had similar experiences and were willing to share how to deal with them. I also found that I could also be an encouragement to others that were coming behind me and instructing them on the ways to go and not make the same mistakes that I did or feel that same isolation. At minimum, they had me to talk to.

What to do if you are the only one.

- Find a mentor: The search may be long and hard but you must discover someone that you can talk to. It might be an older student that you admire or a teacher or someone in your community that has a similar passion as you. That way you will not feel so disconnected and distracted by being one of a few.

- Find a mentee: Know and recognize the position that you are in. Remember it and understand that there is someone behind you that might be feeling the same way. Reach out to that person and be an encouragement for them. You guys can be a support for each other.

Don't feel that you must over impress. You know what you know. You do not have to do tricks for anyone. Eventually, people will come around and appreciate you.

Embracing a gift

Why did I want to compile this book? As I started thinking through a myriad of thoughts, I reflected a lot on my youth. I realized it took me way too long to embrace my intelligence and fighting against a gift that was bestowed on me. As a youth, I gave in to the peer pressure that if you were smart, you were not allowed to be anything else. You were placed in this bucket and that was the only bucket you could exist in. But as I grew older, I began to realize that it is not necessary to be just one thing. You can embrace intelligence, be considered attractive, be athletic, and be whatever you wished. You did not have to choose. I embraced my smarts and found my intelligence attractive. Is this the only reason I embraced my gift? Of course not! Embracing smarts had so many other advantages than being considered cute. What I found was that I truly enjoyed the subject of math and numbers and that I was good at analyzing and solving puzzles (which is what math provided for me).

Instead of fighting against the knowledge and struggle against what I would inescapably become. I became more at ease. In wanting to learn more about the subject, I became better. I found myself so much happier when I allowed myself to engulf polynomials, see the slippery slope of slopes, calibrate the probability of probability, understand the geometry of shapes, and ultimately derive the derivative of derivatives. It all became fascinating and I just wanted to embrace as much of it as I could. I was no longer torn and just found it liberating when I finally understood that I could be me and all that entails.

How to Embrace

- Just do. It is okay to like the subjects you like.
- You can have it all. You can have both beauty and brains. I always thought that if you were smart then you could not be cute. Well, let me tell you something intelligence is even more attractive.

In the following pages, you are going to be introduced to eleven young ladies who have embraced their STEM passions. Reading through their submissions brings my heart immense joy; to see how far we have come in young girl's excitement in STEM. I find it really inspiring how soon they have each embraced their STEM smarts. This book was created to encourage young ladies to embrace their intelligence in the STEM fields. There are others who have found an appreciation in these fields and there is a need. I hope that they will also be an encouragement to you.

What are Alexis' responses to the same questions?

I had each of the young ladies respond to several questions. I also want to give you a peek into my psyche and answer many of the same questions.

- **Why do you like the STEM field(s) that you like?**

  - I like that mathematics is static. There are several ways to get to an answer but there is only one answer. There is no subjectivity to it. If I asked you to define the slope of the line $y = 3x + 8$. There are at least 4 different ways that you can give me the one answer of 3. I also like the puzzle aspect to mathematics meaning something to solve or put together to get a complete picture. When I am doing a Geometry proof, I like how the evidences lines up (pieces come together) to prove the conclusion.

- **Taking this STEM passion, what do you envision yourself becoming (i.e. your ultimate career goal)?**

  o My ultimate career goals have morphed a lot throughout the years. When I was, younger I wanted to be a photographer. As I grew into my love of numbers and puzzles, I wanted to be an accountant. When I started work at MIT Lincoln Laboratories, I enjoyed the process of coding and creating something from an idea and I always enjoyed teaching. My ultimate goal was to be a Triple E: educator, entrepreneur, and engineer.

- **Have you ever been afraid to show people how smart you are in your chosen STEM field? If so, how do you deal with that?**

  o When I was younger yes. I did not deal with that well. My solution was to hide and that left me feeling miserable. That is the main purpose for this book. I really would like young ladies to not have the same fears that I had. It took me a long time lose that fear and embrace the gift I was given. Once I lost the fear and truly embraced the gift, I was a lot happier.

- **When did you first realize that you liked your STEM subject?**

  o I think I first realized I had a passion for math during my freshman year in college. I always had a passion for numbers and puzzles as a young girl. I enjoyed Geometry and Calculus in high school, but I did not associate that with "mathematics". I just saw it something interesting to do. Another puzzle that needed solving. During my freshman year of college, I began tutoring in the mathematics lab and taking college math courses and found a fascination with the subject. Mathematics was more than just solving puzzles, there was a beauty in the theory of how the numbers and the calculations worked and I had a desire to learn more.

- **What would you tell another young lady who is coming to grips with her passion for STEM but afraid to fully embrace it?**

  o I would suggest they learn from me and not wait to come to grips with the love of their STEM subject. You are wasting time, effort, and energy. It takes way more effort to deny that passion than it does to fully embrace it. You will not be fully happy until you embrace what you enjoy.

- **Who is your biggest STEM influence and why?**

  o I have had many a mentor/influence throughout my career. Many my professors at Spelman College I regard highly. Dr. Julia Thompson, a Physics Professor from the University of Pittsburgh, was a huge influence on me. Prior to her, I never knew a female physics scientist. For me just seeing these women in such high positions and with such expanse of knowledge and holding their own in their respective fields which were usually populated by men was impressive.

- **What would you like to see more of in the STEM field?**

  o I would like to see a more diversity in STEM field. I would like to walk into meetings and not be the only one or one of two at the big table. I would like to see more women and minorities represented.

- **Do you ever feel challenged in your STEM area that you have chosen? Do you often feel that you have to "prove yourself "? I.e. do you feel that people do not respect your intelligence?**

  o I have felt challenged since I graduated from undergrad. I always feel that I must do extra to prove myself. You know prove that I deserve that 100 on the test. But the hoops I used to jump through and the tricks I used to perform, I don't do those now. Because I don't need to. People generally understand that I know what I am doing.

- **Is there anything that you would change at your school that you believe would help encourage more girls into the area of STEM?**

  o Looking at it now, I see schools developing more programs to encourage women and minorities into the STEM fields. This is a huge advancement than when I started out.

- **Name the last STEM project that you worked on that you were genuinely excited about? Why?**

  o I have worked on several STEM projects that I have brought me genuine joy. My current experiences as an entrepreneur in offering tutoring in STEM subjects and seeing young girls embrace those sessions have brought a huge excitement. This book project, which is evolving into an entire series, has brought a huge excitement. Stay tuned ☺

ALEXIS M. SCOTT

Alexis M. Scott is a Triple E: Educator, Entrepreneur, and Engineer. She founded AMS Academic Solutions to share her gift of numbers and education that she has possessed since an early age. She has been teaching Mathematics for over 20 years including 18 years as a college professor. She is a 2017 NSBE Hidden Figures Awards recipient for her contributions in STEM. She currently lives in Dallas, TX and in her spare time enjoys playing tennis.

Contact Alexis Scott @ alexis@amsacademicsolutions.com or visit her website: www.amsacademicsolutions.com.

One way to keep momentum going is to have constantly greater goals.

Michael Korda

ALEXANDRA "ALLIE" FRYMIRE

Why do you like the STEM field(s) that you like?

I love physics because every phenomenon (of course save for the Standard Model of elementary particles) follows a strict set of rules. Scientists create physical laws and equations with consistent universal application as their top priority. Given how much structure and rule following I demand in my own life, it's easy to see why a subject like physics appeals so much to me. It feels like less of an academic obligation and more of an exploration into my own thought process and how to solve complex problems using my way of thinking.

Taking this STEM passion, what do you envision yourself becoming (i.e. your ultimate career goal)?

I want to be on the front lines of astrophysics and cosmology working with the world's leading physicists uncovering the universe's deepest and darkest secrets that have yet to be revealed. Astrophysics is incredibly intriguing to me, and I hope to pursue it further throughout my education and career.

Have you ever been afraid to show people how smart you are in your chosen STEM field? If so, how do you deal with that?

I'm not afraid to engage in the discussion in a way that demonstrates my intelligence or my confidence, but I don't go out of my way to show that I'm the smartest or have the highest scores. I feel more comfortable keeping those things to myself.

When did you first realize that you liked your STEM subject?

I first realized that I wanted to pursue physics last summer, when I took an honors physics course so I could move ahead to more advanced courses the following school year. Although I went into the online class knowing that physics would be something I'd enjoy, the actual experience of class itself only further proved my prediction and drove me toward a deeper, more enriched passion for physics.

What would you tell another young lady who is coming to grips with her passion for STEM but afraid to fully embrace it?

Find something that inspires you; a teacher, a lofty goal or even just a grade, and keep that in mind whenever you doubt yourself. When you don't feel confident, you must keep going. You may doubt yourself, feel unconfident, or think you are the least intelligent person in the room, but don't stop. Even if you're alone now, keep going, so that the girls who come after you don't have to be alone.

Who is your biggest STEM influence and why?

My AP Calculus BC teacher, Mrs. Falk, has been a big inspiration to me. She always seems so confident in my ability to conquer higher levels of math, which encourages me to think bigger and realize that I can do important things with math. Whenever I turn in my tests, she always asks me "Is this my answer key?" and even if I think I did poorly, her attitude gives me an extra boost of confidence in my work and intelligence.

What would you like to see more of in the STEM field?

I would love to see more hands-on, physical science in extracurricular activities for girls. Boys learn engineering and science in almost everything they are offered, and I would like to see the same for girls. If we do this, then fewer young women and girls will be discouraged from science, especially physics, and further close the gender gap in STEM.

Do you ever feel challenged in your STEM area that you have chosen?

Yes! All the time. The concepts are difficult, so I must work hard and study a lot to make sure I truly understand them. In AP Physics C, where I'm the only girl, I'm often hesitant to ask for help when I need it and be thought of as not good enough. This creates additional obstacles in an already challenging course load.

Is there anything that you would change at your school that you believe would help encourage more girls into the area of STEM?

At my school, I want to revamp the upper school science department. There are no upper school female science teachers teaching advanced classes, and often the other male teachers seem indifferent to the lack of female representation in our most advanced science courses. They say that, somehow, it is not their responsibility to resolve these problems as they cannot control how many girls register for classes. However, I believe that by reflecting on and taking accountability for this gender gap by encouraging female voices and female students to be interested in more advanced science, would really help uplift not only students but also the entire department.

Do you often feel that you have to "prove yourself "? I.e. do you feel that people do not respect your intelligence?

All the time! Especially in my classes where I am the only girl. I feel as though I must go the extra mile to really prove my intellectual worth, even though I've already established myself as an academic leader in the class. It can be very frustrating to feel as though I must represent all women interested in a particular subject, and yet my intelligence goes frequently unacknowledged.

Name the last STEM project that you worked on that you were genuinely excited about? Why?

In my Problem-Solving class, we are currently working on a project with a local investment firm to use mathematical modeling to optimize the portfolios of their clients. It has been very interesting to finally see the real-world applications of topics we've been learning about in theory throughout most the year.

ALEXANDRA "ALLIE" FRYMIRE

I'm a varsity volleyball captain and state champion, the only girl captain of the math team and the only girl in AP Physics C. Before all that, and for as long as I can remember, I've had an intense passion for math. In high school, I discovered one of math's most beautiful applications: physics. I hope to study physics, especially astrophysics, and bring more female voices, including mine, into the field of physics in the future.

Alexandra "Allie" Frymire / Greenhill School / Class of 2018

Whatever you can do, or dream you can, begin it.

Boldness has genius, power and magic in it.

Johann Wolfgang von Goethe

MARY MULCAHY

Why do you like the STEM field(s) that you like?

What I like most about STEM fields in general is that they deal with universal truths, not feelings or opinions. Specifically, I like biology and engineering (and will be majoring in Biomedical Engineering at Georgia Tech in the fall). Biology helps us understand ourselves. We are a complex and beautiful machine of millions of systems working together in flawless collaboration. I want to learn about how things interact with each other and all the complex and dazzling systems that all must be working in perfect unison and teamwork to keep our bodies running. Engineering teaches you how to solve complicated problems and think analytically about the world.

Taking this STEM passion, what do you envision yourself becoming (i.e. your ultimate career goal)?

Ultimately, I want to be a research scientist in the cancer field. It is my specific career goal to develop a more advanced and less invasive way to diagnose cancer, so that it can be detected and treated earlier and increase the likelihood of survival.

To accomplish this, I plan to major in Biomedical Engineering, take the required pre-med coursework, and ultimately obtain a Masters, then a PhD. To appropriately prepare me for this pursuit, I have taken every advanced math and science course offered at my high school and interned with a highly-respected cancer surgeon.

Have you ever been afraid to show people how smart you are in your chosen STEM field? If so, how do you deal with that?

My high school is extremely competitive. If you demonstrate that you are smart, regardless of your gender, you essentially put a target on your back. Being in the top 10% is required for consideration for honors and auto-admit for some colleges. In general, my theory is to fly under the radar. I'm not necessarily afraid of showing off, but I'm humble. So yes, I don't show people how smart I am in STEM, but I don't show people how smart I am in anything, because I was raised to not make myself out to be better than other people.

That's why I really enjoy tutoring in science so much. Since I am tutoring the subject, I'm expected to be smart in it and I get to show off my scientific knowledge, (like knowing periodic elements and their molar masses off the top of my head) while helping others. My kids know how smart I am, and that's good enough for me.

When did you first realize that you liked your STEM subject?

I wish I could say that I've known I wanted to pursue STEM since I was a young girl, or that it came to me in a dream one night. But honestly, I didn't know that I wanted to study STEM until after my freshman year of high school.

High school is a time to find yourself and experiment with new things (hobbies and intellectual interests mind you, not drugs). Psychologically, teenagers are just entering the formal operational developmental stage of their lives, where they can think critically, form their own opinions, and make decisions for themselves. Thus, it is critical to seize the opportunities high school presents to find yourself and discover what you are passionate about.

Throughout my years of schooling, I have taken a multitude of classes in history and writing and literature, but I realized that they just weren't for me. It wasn't until my sophomore year, well into my second year of biology, that I truly realized that I was passionate about science. I was fortunate enough to have articulate and inspiring instructors in biology (and chemistry), which likely helped develop my love for science.

What would you tell another young lady who is coming to grips with her passion for STEM but afraid to fully embrace it?

As cliché as it sounds, I would tell her to believe in herself and not give up. I know that for me the hardest part of pursuing a STEM education was remembering how much I loved it throughout the bad grades and long nights of studying. When the going gets tough, you've got to just keep on going.

As I keep saying, I absolutely LOVE biology, but throughout high school, those courses have been some of my worst grades, because they are very hard. This can be especially disheartening because bad grades and negative feedback have a more profound impact on women than on men. Psychologically, girls have a larger limbic system and amygdala, which are the emotional centers of the brain. Thus, when a girl is given the same negative feedback (for example in the form of a poor grade), she is more likely to take it to heart and become discouraged and doubt her abilities.

That's why it's so critical to constantly remind your STEM sisters to keep their head up and power through, because we all know

STEM classes are hard (for everyone), but the hardest part is keeping your confidence.

Who is your biggest STEM influence and why?

You wouldn't expect a bunch of teenage softball players to call their coach "The Professor." Yet this nickname perfectly suited my father, as he explained to the team the physics behind the perfect swing and invented gadgets to correct imperfect form.

There is no problem too big or too small for him to tackle. When I tried telling him that I simply couldn't ride my bike while lugging a 20-pound softball bag AND a backpack (which seemed like a perfectly reasonable excuse to get out of *biking* to *high school*), he simply removed the retractable handle from an old suitcase and created an extendable shelf on the back of my bike. While solving the issue, this did not make me happy.

My father is the quintessential engineer, starting his own engineering company, and spending every waking moment building something or finding a unique way to solve an obscure problem, either at his office or at our house. My family has always joked that nothing is truly ours until my dad has taken it apart and "improved" it. He has always taught me "that doesn't exist" isn't a valid excuse. If you need something, you can make it happen.

It is this creative, go-getter mentality that has inspired me to pursue engineering. Unlike many students these days, I desire to be a problem solver, not a problem creator. I want to be a catalyst in creating a world where science can alleviate suffering.

What would you like to see more of in the STEM field?

The obvious answer here is, "I would like to see more women in STEM fields." Well, duh. But more specifically, I would like to see more STEM programming at younger ages, which would, in turn, lead to more women in STEM fields. First, I think it's important to do this so that science and math can be introduced to kids at an age before they start worrying about grades and GPA. They can see STEM as fun and exciting, not a letter grade.

Secondly, younger aged programming would help build confidence in these fields earlier, so that when these kids do hit the crazy hard high school classes, they have a sound base to build upon and a confidence in themselves. This baseline confidence is exactly what I see in helping more women excel in the STEM fields, because all students, boys and girls, are required to take biology, chemistry, physics, and algebra II in high school, but the hard part is *keeping* the students in those fields beyond what is just required.

Do you ever feel challenged in your STEM area that you have chosen?

I constantly feel challenged in STEM. Not just because engineering is going to be hard, but because science is always advancing, and as scholars, we must keep up with it and be constantly learning new things.

Just this year, when I was tutoring some kids in biology, I learned how much the curriculum had been updated since I took the course a mere three years ago, when discussing the different methods of blood typing.

That's why I love it so much, because it is so challenging. I'm always learning and I'm always right at the cutting edge of what science has to offer, like the entire world is full of untapped potential.

Is there anything that you would change at your school that you believe would help encourage more girls into the area of STEM?

At my school, very few people, male or female, pursue STEM careers. I think my school needs to work on encouraging *everyone* to pursue STEM. At many schools, including my own, I feel issues with STEM education are often overlooked. My school throws a parade when the football team wins state, but not when the Academic Decathlon team does. The best coaches get hired instead of, for example, the best pre-calculus teachers. Having a bad math or science teacher can really discourage students. These subjects build on each other, and a bad experience will cause students to just give up.

The obvious answer is to really focus on hiring the best, most passionate, encouraging teachers in math and science. That is, however, not always possible, so the next best thing would be to augment teaching with a support network of tutoring, practice sessions, and counseling from former students - because these classes can be hard even with a fabulous teacher.

Do you often feel that you have to "prove yourself "? I.e. do you feel that people do not respect your intelligence?

Imagine walking into a class on your first day of school and having a teacher tell you, "Women are as dumb as rocks." This experience happened to my mother in one of her classes in college, and in response, she felt the need to have a man ask the professor her high-level questions (she was an engineering major so there was an abundance of men present to do the job).

This blatant disrespect that my mother endured inspired me to never take that from anybody. It motivated me to always stand up for myself before anyone could put me down and make me feel like I had to prove myself. Sadly, sometimes there are instances where you need to put some people in their place when they try to belittle your intelligence.

For example, on my last Organic Chemistry project, a group of two boys and I were tasked with explaining the different mechanisms of alkene addition reactions (crazy hard stuff). After becoming an expert on the subject and developing a presentation, I overheard the two male counterparts of my group discussing our presentation- telling each other, "Ok, you talk about the first part, I'll talk about the second, and Mary can stand there and look pretty." Obviously, I was planning on looking pretty, but he was *brutally* mistaken if he thought I didn't have anything else to contribute to the group. The next day, when he was presenting incomplete and incorrect information to the class, I stopped him and explained how it really went. The class applauded.

However, this is not to say that you should ever have to prove yourself when someone belittles you. Be it a man or a woman who denigrates you, it is important to remember that you don't owe anything to that person. If they don't respect you, then they don't deserve your effort to impress them.

Name the last STEM project that you worked on that you were genuinely excited about? Why?

This past summer, as part of my Girl Scout Gold Award, I organized and taught a biology and chemistry camp for over 60 underprivileged middle schoolers in West Dallas. I set up a miniature bio-lab classroom, complete with 10 microscopes and prepared slides, and presented a multiple-day seminar. Bringing high school student volunteers to help with the microscopes, I taught the children about the wonders of the biological and chemical sciences. After creating a website for the camp with detailed instructional and explanatory videos and camp information, I donated the purchased microscopes and remaining supplies to the organization so that subsequent children can enjoy the science experiments at the camp for years to come. Although my camp initially helped around 60 students, it will eventually impact hundreds of children, as the organization continues to teach after-school and summer camps each year and will be able to use the curriculum and supplies.

Through my camp, the students were introduced to science in a way that was fun and enjoyable for them. They looked at their own cheek cells under the microscope, made an egg bounce, made slime, looked at microscopic parasites, and participated in many other engaging activities. The most exciting part of this experience for me was the obvious positive impact it had on the students. For example, one student brought a tiny digital camera to take pictures through the microscopes. Another said he wished my science camp was there every day. Some were thinking more deeply about science and going beyond what I presented to them, asking me questions like, "What's the difference between regular ice and dry ice?" and using their free time to pull their hair out to look at the follicles under the microscope.

I ran this camp in West Dallas, an area with one of the highest child poverty rates in the country; where less than half of the 9th graders who start high school go on to earn their diploma. Initially, few of these children aspire to become a doctor or an engineer. What affected me the most from this experience was the students' responses in a post camp survey, where almost all the students indicated that this camp made them want to pursue a further education and career in the STEM (Science, Technology, Engineering, and Math) field.

Following the startling results of my camp, I decided to continue running it every summer, not for any awards, but merely to spread the fun of STEM learning. I will be teaching it myself again this summer, and training counselors to manage it for the next years after I go to college.

MARY MULCAHY

My name is Mary Mulcahy and I'm a high school senior at Highland Park High School, Dallas, TX. My passion is cellular-biology and I plan to study Biomedical Engineering.

More than anything I love helping people, and I spend my free-time tutoring refugees and dyslexic children. My dream is to use science to help disabled veterans.

Life shrinks or expands in proportion to one's courage.

Anais Nin

QUINN LANGFORD

Why do you like the STEM field(s) that you like?

I have been exposed to computer science and mechanical engineering from being on a robotics team. When I build things, it makes me feel powerful. When our designs work, I feel accomplished.

Programming has been very mind-opening to me because I have learned how a robot thinks, and what goes on behind the scenes. A background in programming is essential to anyone going into a field that has to do with computers or robots. My dream right now is to go into nanotechnology, which deals with the manipulation of singular atoms and molecules. Using nanotechnology, you could make waterproof Nano-pants, or craft a steak with nothing but the atoms found in protein, or fight cancer. It's a relatively new but diverse field, and these cool and/or important uses of nanotechnology are what interest me.

Taking this STEM passion, what do you envision yourself becoming (i.e. your ultimate career goal)?

I would like to research things related to nanotechnology. I've seen multiple clean rooms, which are rooms that have an extremely low level of environmental pollutants like dust, typically used for scientific research and the manufacturing of products, such as semiconductors. I'm not sure about the specifics of what aspect of nanotechnology I want to research, but I know I imagine myself experimenting with microscopic objects in a clean room.

Have you ever been afraid to show people how smart you are in your chosen STEM field? If so, how do you deal with that?

I was shy when I first joined my robotics team because I didn't want to mess up. Even people who know what they're doing have accidents. Now I'm less shy, and I make a lot of mistakes. But everyone else does, too, and most mistakes are an easy fix, so it's okay. Being less shy was a slow process, and it mostly happened because I made more friendships with people on the team who I felt comfortable around. Even though it took a while for me to open up, I now feel more confident in all aspects of my life, even in situations that aren't so comfortable.

When did you first realize that you liked your STEM subject?

I first learned about nanotechnology in seventh grade because my Gateway to Technology teacher told the class about it. I've had an interest in STEM in general since elementary school, which was inspired by my parents, and fortified by the robotics team that I joined in sixth grade.

What would you tell another young lady who is coming to grips with her passion for STEM but afraid to fully embrace it?

I would tell her to reconsider her priorities. In twenty years, no one will remember the clothes they wore in school or the drama that happened. What sticks with you and impacts your life is the knowledge you get. Whatever or whoever is holding her back is not as important as pursuing her passion and learning as much as she can.

Who is your biggest STEM influence and why?

My biggest STEM influences are my parents, who both studied engineering. Their lives show me that STEM is a path to having a successful and fulfilling life.

What would you like to see more of in the STEM field?

I would like to see more diversity in STEM in general. Every race, religion, gender, etc. should be represented. Every background gives people different view on life, which leads to unique ideas. No one should be excluded from STEM because the world needs every solution to its problems that it can get.

Do you ever feel challenged in your STEM area that you have chosen?

Engineering requires a lot of critical thinking and problem solving. Programming is mostly troubleshooting and debugging. These things can be tough, but every challenge is an opportunity to grow and learn. Plus, despite the difficult parts, STEM activities are very fun.

Is there anything that you would change at your school that you believe would help encourage more girls into the area of STEM?

I wish we had a FIRST (For Inspiration and Recognition of Science and Technology) Robotics team at my school. It could be a club or part of a class. Teams from all over the world compete in FIRST, and the experience teaches young people not only how to build and program a robot, but also how to cooperate with others and have responsibility.

Do you often feel that you have to "prove yourself "? I.e. do you feel that people do not respect your intelligence?

In school, I only answer questions when I 132% know the answer. Some kids just say whatever's on their mind, but I never like to be wrong. My robotics team, which is an all-girls team, has encountered many snide comments. One time, the volunteers asked for help from the team members. Of course, our team was happy to help, but they rejected us because they "needed people who could lift heavy boxes." Other people have asked how we pick up our own robot. I'm lucky that I'm on an all-girls team, though. Most teams only have two or three girls. Every time something bad happens, the boys on the team think, "Oh, that's because we let a girl do that." A double standard is set and girls must be perfect if they want to keep their spot on the team, while boys can make a lot of mistakes. All of this makes me extra proud that my robotics team has overcome adversity in our field to become a widely-respected competitor.

Name the last STEM project that you worked on that you were genuinely excited about? Why?

Every year my robotics team works together to build a robot in six weeks that completes certain tasks to earn points in a competition. This past year, we had to design a robot that would shoot whiffle balls into a goal, carry and place gears, and climb a rope. Our robot could do all of that, and we also built another one that was its identical twin. I'm proud of these robots because we built them from scratch. Every single piece was designed and cut by a kid. I was excited about it because competing is fun, and the accomplishment that I feel every time we finish is one of the best feelings in the world.

QUINN LANGFORD

Quinn Langford is a high school freshman and a member of FIRST Robotics Competition Team 2881, The Lady Cans. Building and programming FIRST robots has given her the opportunity to learn about STEM in a fun way. As her team's Director of Outreach, she inspires youth to become STEM leaders.

Strive not to be a success, but rather to be of value.

Albert Einstein

DESTINY SIMONE ADAMS

Name the last STEM project that you worked on that you were genuinely excited about? Why?

I recently completed my 1st game design using Scratch. I was genuinely excited because it was a very complex game to code requiring precision and accuracy. I completed this game in 2 weeks with the help of my Girls Who Code mentors. I initially thought it would be easy however I am glad I chose this because I learned a lot about persistence and gained new skills.

Do you often feel that you have to "prove yourself "? I.e. do you feel that people do not respect your intelligence?

I always feel like I must constantly prove myself to others in the STEM field. I am a double minority and this makes it even more difficult. As an African American female in STEM, it is a challenge to be treated equally. My opinion and or ideas are often ignored or sometimes rarely considered. In those cases, I always fight to prove my worth and remain confident in my contributions.

Is there anything that you would change at your school that you believe would help encourage more girls into the area of STEM?

I'm fortunate to attend a STEAM based school and there are resources however the information is not always equally shared amongst all students. As a freshman, I've had to really search to find new opportunities within the school. I also wish more events were held at our school to help expose girls to the various career fields in

STEM. Lastly, I wish our clubs were more active and involved in outside events.

Do you ever feel challenged in your STEM area that you have chosen?

Computer Science major is challenging. My biggest challenge is the ability to focus on one aspect of this major, considering there are a plethora of things to learn. For example, I find myself starting new projects & exploring new programming languages before completing the previous ones. It makes it harder to master a skill effectively doing this.

What would you like to see more of in the STEM field?

I would like to see more minority girls accept the challenges within the STEAM field. It can be rewarding once you overcome the barriers. It will also be more comfortable for everyone considering that we will not be experiencing these obstacles alone. I think that it is important to have more minority girls in the STEM field because it is very uncommon and it isn't expected of us.

What would you tell another young lady who is coming to grips with her passion for STEM but afraid to fully embrace it?

I would tell her to not be fearful of pursuing her passion. The learning experience can be scary but if it's something she truly enjoys; she should strive to be successful. There are many people available that are willing to support & guide her along the journey.

When did you first realize that you liked your STEM subject?

My 1st experience in which I discovered my love for science occurred in 6th grade. My teacher made the subject enjoyable, easy to understand & exciting. During that same year, I took a course in Business & Computer Science. In this course, we studied the introduction to coding & basic computing skills. These courses were very impactful & where my love for STEM began.

Have you ever been afraid to show people how smart you are in your chosen STEM?

Honestly, I've never been afraid or shameful of my interest in STEM! I don't focus on what people think about my career choice instead I embrace this as my happy place. I'm hopeful that this approach helps others who are afraid to show their interest & given talents. Just shine!

Taking this STEM passion, what do you envision yourself becoming (i.e. your ultimate career goal)?

I envision myself as a computer scientist. I chose this field because I enjoy solving complex problems using technology. This field allows me to expand my creativity & uniqueness.

Why do you like the STEM field(s) that you like?

I like the computer science field because it allows me to contribute to an end product that can be pleasing & useful to others. I like to see people happy with the finished product. This makes me feel joyful because I've helped someone or something else positively. Overall, I love solving problems.

Who is your biggest STEM influence and why?

Barbara Liskov is my biggest influencer in STEM! Her original career was to become a mathematician however her later interests landed her a career as a computer scientist. Her ability to remain confident and not let others intimidate her is impressive to me!

DESTINY SIMONE ADAMS

Yes, I'm that girl.
The World Traveler.
Inspiring Computer Scientist.
High achiever and God Believer.
I'm the girl that has her head held up
high and is reaching for the sky.
For now I'm
The Nerd
The Geek
The Bookworm
Someday I'll run things, come along
with me.
- Destiny Adams

North Springs Charter High School
Sandy Springs, Georgia

Whatever the mind of man can conceive and believe, it can achieve.

Napoleon Hill

AVA BARRETT-SCOTT

Why do you like the STEM field(s) that you like?

I like the "science" part of STEM, since there is a health aspect to it and it can help me study for my aspiring career as a dermatologist.

Have you ever been afraid to show people how smart you are in your chosen STEM field? If so, how do you deal with that?

I am never afraid to show people how smart I am because intelligence expresses great accomplishments. However, many people do underestimate how smart I am and it can be challenging. It can be challenging because a lot of the times people explain to me over and over things I already know, when I could be using that time to learn things that I do not know.

When did you first realize that you liked your STEM subject?

I realized I first liked the science part of STEM when I began to gain interest in the subject beginning at the age of seven. Science has also helped me gain great conclusions in my daily life about our solar system, biology, and health. It has helped me with these conclusions by helping me incorporate what I already know about these things, and then using a scientific aspect on it from the knowledge I have learned and already know.

What would you tell another young lady who is coming to grips with her passion for STEM but afraid to fully embrace it?

I would tell her that she can achieve remarkable things if she fully embraces what she loves, with no hesitation. Being a lady in a STEM field is not as common as being a male in the STEM field. The more ladies embrace the STEM field, the more other females are inspired to join as well.

Who is your biggest STEM influence and why?

My biggest influence in STEM is my science teacher, since I learned the most about the science field in her class. It has helped me to use more of the scientific aspect of things in my daily education.

What would you like to see more of in the STEM field?

I would like to see more "health type" things in the STEM field. What type of things do you want to see? For people like me who want to become a doctor of some sort, or who are interested in anything in the health field at all.

Do you ever feel challenged in your STEM area that you have chosen?

Sometimes, I do feel a little challenged in science, but it helps me to become better at it once I learn the things I do not understand. However, there is nothing I cannot handle, and it is not too overwhelming.

Is there anything that you would change at your school that you believe would help encourage more girls into the area of STEM?

I think making girls more aware at school about the opportunities and benefits they have when joining the STEM program will help them be more aware of the possibilities. Also, acknowledging that it is okay as a girl to be interested in STEM and you can accomplish whatever you want with courage and motivation, no matter what gender you are.

Do you often feel that you have to "prove yourself "? I.e. do you feel that people do not respect your intelligence?

I often feel like I do have to prove myself, because I am not only a female, but someone who some say don't "look like they're smart". However, comments like those help me strive to do better, and show others that I can do things that they claim I am not capable of doing.

Name the last STEM project that you worked on that you were genuinely excited about? Why?

The last project that I was excited about was in science about biomes. You got to choose the biome you did and give information on it like the climate, organisms, etc. That project excited me because I got to use my creativity. I decorated the posteron the aspects of the biome that I chose to do and expressed my creativity in a scientific way.

Taking this STEM passion, what do you envision yourself becoming (i.e. your ultimate career goal)?

My ultimate career goal is to become a dermatologist, or a skin specialist. I know with both careers there is a lot of science and logic involved, with a mix of health education and the ability to make good conclusions. With the science and health information I have learned to date, STEM will help me thrive in being a dermatologist, or any kind of doctor or physician.

AVA BARRETT-SCOTT

My name is Ava Barrett-Scott, and I am a 13-year-old female student at Liberty Junior High in Dallas, Texas where I was born and raised. I have a passion for playing competitive volleyball but my aspiration soon in life is to become a dermatologist, and a cosmetologist on the side.

My favorite subject is science, because it helps me combine common sense with knowledge on the things I learn in science. The health part of science also interests me greatly, considering the future career I would like to do. Science also has some creative parts to it, like when you need to think outside the box to solve an investigation, or find out why someone is sick, and a cure for that illness. I encourage anyone around my age to recognize the many opportunities you have ahead of you when you learn about careers in the science field, or more importantly, STEM. I especially encourage other young ladies to pursue something in these fields, not only because you are interested in them, but to show others that even as a young lady you can accomplish stuff that most males are in. And that you can take the criticism you get, and thrive greatly from it, to prove to others what you can do.

Definiteness of purpose is the starting point of all achievement.

W. Clement Stone

JAZZELINE CAGER

Why do you like the STEM field(s) that you like?

The reason I love science is because, I love creating formulas to get certain reactions, such as an explosion. I love realizing that I made that happen. As a tween girl, I am always on my phone and computer; this is the reason that I love technology. I love to build websites and apps and publishing them to the internet to get their reactions. I enjoy engineering because, I love seeing the newest robots being released, or a rocket being launched into the sky. I enjoy knowing that a woman could've possibly helped release the rocket into the sky or programmed the robot to tell you the weather; knowing that empowers me.

Taking this STEM passion, what do you envision yourself becoming (i.e. your ultimate career goal)?

I know that everybody has a God given gift. As a scientist, I want my career to empower a young girl who has not discovered her love for the STEM fields. I envision myself becoming a scientist that the entire world knows and I want to create cures for diseases in the future.

Have you ever been afraid to show people how smart you are in your chosen STEM field? If so, how do you deal with that?

I wouldn't say that I was afraid to show my passion for STEM, but I do think that I hid it for a while for the sake of my friends.

While they were playing with dolls, I was reading the science books, and they didn't understand why I wasn't playing with them. I loved playing with dolls, but I realized that I could play with dolls anytime. I wanted to read science books at school. For a while, I didn't tell them how much I loved STEM, and I stopped reading those books and started doing what they were doing. When I began homeschooling I felt free from hiding my passion and finally embraced my STEM passion.

When did you first realize that you liked your STEM subject?

In kindergarten, my teacher told us that we were going to make a volcano. When the day came for us to make the volcano, I saw the reaction of the baking soda and vinegar, and that was the exact moment that I knew that science was a subject that I wanted to fully embrace.

What would you tell another young lady who is coming to grips with her passion for STEM but afraid to fully embrace it?

We were all born with a purpose, for some it's to paint, for others it's cooking; for me, it's STEM. This may be the same purpose for her. I would tell her to join a group of other people who also love the STEM field for some moral support, and to just go for it. Nothing should stop her from fully embracing her passion.

Who is your biggest STEM influence and why?

Katherine Johnson. She's my biggest STEM influence because, when everybody else thought she couldn't do powerful things such as doing the math to shoot John Glenn onto the moon, she did it and proved them all wrong. I also had a science teacher who made science fun, and I think that's a very important quality in a science teacher.

What would you like to see more of in the STEM field?

I would love to see more African American women study science and engineering or any other field they choose.

Do you ever feel challenged in your STEM area that you have chosen?

Yes! I definitely feel challenged in science and technology, especially when I take computer classes. When I get too frustrated, I take a break and pray about it, and it seems every time I come back, from my break it gets a little easier.

Is there anything that you would change at your school that you believe would help encourage more girls into the area of STEM?

As a homeschooled student myself, I want to see more homeschool programs that focus on STEM, in particular girls in STEM. I would create a Girls in STEM homeschool class for girls like me.

Do you often feel that you have to "prove yourself "? I.e. do you feel that people do not respect your intelligence?

Yes, I do feel that I must prove myself. For example, if I were in a volcano competition, and someone made a larger volcano than what I made, I would want to make a larger volcano than theirs and write a whole lesson on volcanoes. I don't feel that people do not respect my intelligence, however, I do not like when people say, "Are you sure that's what you like?" because unlike some people, I do understand myself and my interests.

Name the last STEM project that you worked on that you were genuinely excited about? Why?

I am currently working on a homemade solar oven, which is a device that you cook food in and leave it in the sun for it to cook thoroughly. If all goes well, I might start cooking all my food in the sun, but that's just the scientist in me.

JAZZELINE CAGER

Jazzeline is 11 and a 5th grade homeschooler. She loves God and spending time with her family. Jazz is co-owner of A Child At heART School and loves expressing herself through painting, writing, singing, dancing and fashion. Jazzeline aspires to become a scientist and an engineer someday because STEM rocks!

The only person you are destined to become is the person you decide to be.

Ralph Waldo Emerson

ELIZABETH CARSON

Why do you like the STEM fields that you like?

There are a couple of reasons I really like the STEM fields of math and technology. In both areas, I get to figure things out, solve problems, and learn innovative ways to approach problems. With technology, I enjoy making and editing my own videos. By doing that, I get to be creative.

Taking this STEM passion, what do you envision yourself becoming (i.e. your ultimate career goal)?

I have considered becoming a math teacher because I really enjoy helping people, and I like figuring out math problems. Last year, at the end of 6th grade, I received a perfect score on the math section of the California state tests.

Have you ever been afraid to show people how smart you are in your chosen STEM field? If so, how do you deal with that?

I was embarrassed for people to know that because I'm already known as a "smart girl" in school. Now, in 7th grade, I embrace my capacity in math, but I don't try to draw attention to myself. My teachers often ask me to help other students in my math class with their assignments, and I'm willing to help. It makes me feel good to be able to help one of my peers understand math better.

When did you first realize that you liked your STEM subject?

I was about 10 years old when I first realized I enjoyed editing videos. Now I really admire the technology and video editing of Casey Neistat because of the artistic and unique way he edits his videos.

Who is your biggest STEM influence and why?

It wasn't until about this year that I realized I enjoy math. Part of that has to do with both my 6th and 7th grade math teachers. Mrs. Nakano, in 6th grade, and Mr. Villegas, this year in 7th grade, are both very good at teaching math because they fully explain what we are learning and how we are going about it. I admire both.

Do you often feel that you have to "prove yourself"?

I don't really feel a lack of respect in terms of my intelligence. If anything, I sometimes feel that people exaggerate my intelligence to the point it's embarrassing. That's when I try to hide my intelligence.

Do you ever feel challenged in your STEM area that you have chosen?

I do feel challenged in videography/technology whenever I'm learning a new video editing software. It's challenging, but at the same time, I enjoy the challenge.

What would you tell another young lady who is coming to grips with her passion for STEM but afraid to fully embrace it?

Everybody has his/her own interests, so if that's what you enjoy, then go for it!

What would you like to see more of in the STEM field?

I would really like to see more ways you can incorporate art and creativity with STEM.

Name the last STEM project that you worked on that you were genuinely excited about? Why?

In my last STEM project, I created a video about my recent trip to Disneyland. I incorporated music, timing, and artistic transitions to make the video more appealing, more interesting, and more enjoyable.

ELIZABETH CARSON

Elizabeth is a 13-year-old from San Diego, CA. She is a 7th grader at Nestor Language Academy Charter School, a Spanish/English dual language immersion program where she has attended since kindergarten. She enjoys swimming, running, playing the violin and being creative.

Go confidently in the direction of your dreams.

Live the life you have imagined.

Henry David Thoreau

SOMMER COTTON

Why do you like the STEM field(s) that you like?

I like math and science because I feel that numbers and equations are fun, enjoyable, and important for many things in life. We use math all the time when we calculate sales tax, income tax, shoe sizes, dress sizes, and so much more. Science is also used in our everyday lives from the food we eat to the soap, shampoo and toothpaste we use in our daily lives.

Taking this STEM passion, what do you envision yourself becoming (i.e. your ultimate career goal)?

My ultimate career goal is to attend Harvard University to become a criminal lawyer. During the investigation of a crime, I plan to use my STEM passion to help gather evidence in a criminal court case. The results of my research will be presented in court to prove that someone is either guilty or innocent.

Have you ever been afraid to show people how smart you are in your chosen STEM field? If so, how do you deal with that?

No. I have never been afraid to show others how smart I am because being smart is a blessing from God. Also, my parents have always built up our (my brother and I) self-confidence when it comes to academic achievements. My dad starting teaching us at an early age about something he called **Triple A**. Triple A stood for Academics, Arts and Athletics. He believed that these three things would help us become well rounded students while maximizing our chances to get a scholarship to college one day.

When did you first realize that you liked your STEM subject?

I realized that I loved math in the 2nd grade when we first started using our multiplication factors. I really enjoyed combining two small numbers to make one BIG number. This reminded me of what it was like when you are working with a team. Everyone can do good things on their own, but as a team, we can accomplish amazing things.

What would you tell another young lady who is coming to grips with her passion for STEM but afraid to fully embrace it?

STEM may not affect your future but it can create a whole new beginning for you. You could be a journalist, actress, or a scientist as long as you're doing what you love and enjoy.

Who is your biggest STEM influence and why?

My parents are my biggest influence. My father because he is an engineer. He always challenges me to figure out the total price on our groceries while standing in the checkout line at Walmart or Kroger before the cashier would give us our total price. This causes me to use lots of mental math. He also enrolled me in the Chinese School of Dallas every summer so that I can continue to challenge myself by taken courses that are above my grade level. It was here that I learned how others were earning academic scholarships to Ivy League schools. My mother is a huge influence on me because she is a teacher. She has a passion for the arts. She also uses technology in her classroom to help the students learn better.

What would you like to see more of in the STEM field?

I would love to see more leaders take charge in the STEM fields. Having more leaders in the classroom can help encourage future bosses. They could create businesses to change the world or simply change their communities.

Do you ever feel challenged in your STEM area that you have chosen?

Of course. Whether I learn something new or something more difficult, there is always a huge challenge. Sometimes, I may or may not always understand the concept, but that drives me to want to work that much harder.

Is there anything that you would change at your school that you believe would help encourage more girls into the area of STEM?

I feel that we could have more girls join STEM at my school by having more club and hands-on activities to influence them. Maybe our school could introduce a STEM club for girls only. I believe this would get girls excited about exploring new things and encourage them to continue the STEM path.

Do you often feel that you have to "prove yourself "? I.e. do you feel that people do not respect your intelligence?

Yes, because of the way I look, the way I dress, the color of my skin, and because of my gender. Others seem to think I'm not as academically gifted as my other classmates. I am always motivated to prove them wrong.

Name the last STEM project that you worked on that you were genuinely excited about? Why?

I really enjoyed when Raytheon came to our school and had us build a catapult system. This project was very exciting because it allowed us to change and manipulate the bolts and screws. I was responsible for my own learning and I had to collaborate with a team to create a product.

After constructing the catapult and reflecting on the experience, my teammates and I brainstormed about ways to improve our system. Maybe the main screw was too high or too low? The experience helped me learn how the location of the screw could affect the distance of the rubber balls in flight.

SOMMER COTTON

My name is Sommer Cotton. I am a sixth-grade Honor Roll student at Cockrill Middle School in McKinney, Texas. I currently have a 3.9 GPA. I enjoy math, science, orchestra, softball and basketball. My free time is spent exploring my creative side through arts and crafts. My future career goals consist of attending law school.

Challenges are what make life interesting and overcoming them is what makes life meaningful.

Joshua J. Marine

AUDREY GUTGSELL

Why do you like the STEM field(s) that you like?

I am adopted from China and so are my brother and sister. I am the oldest of my siblings and when my parents adopted me, they requested a healthy baby girl. When my parents decided to adopt again, my parents requested a baby with special needs. My sister was referred to us and she was born with a cleft lip and palate, which I call an "Open Smile". After adopting my sister, my parents completed our family by requesting to adopt another child with a cleft lip and palate, since they already had experience with this birth difference. To date, my sister has had 17 surgeries and my brother has had 11 surgeries. I have witnessed them being stared at by adults and children alike because of various craniofacial devices they have had to wear.

Additionally, children can be very insensitive and cruel at times. It hurt me to see my sister and brother suffer both physically and emotionally. Despite the challenges they have faced, their attitude is amazing! I am so proud of them. I wanted to write a children's book for other children who have been born with "open smiles", like my sister and brother. I wanted to let them know that they are not alone and that they are true heroes. I also wanted to help children who have been born without "open smiles" to understand some of the challenges these heroes have faced, so for my Girl Scout Gold Award Project I wrote "Open Smiles".

I concluded that technology and medical disabilities are the two categories that appeal to me the most. Math and science weren't exactly subjects that came the easiest for me in school, but the fascination of technology, especially in our world was something that has always impressed me. Having an engineer in my family, that was something that made me feel more comfortable with technology.

Taking this STEM passion, what do you envision yourself becoming (i.e. your ultimate career goal)?

In the future, I've always seen myself pursuing my passion of writing and communicating with others. Though the official career hasn't been decided, I have been considering certain ones such as a journalist, TV broadcaster, visual advertiser, or something involved in public relations. Technology will play a significant role in any of the careers that I choose because I will be required to communicate easily with others and to use technology to help get my opinion and words out there for others to read. I would like to write other children's books for other special medical conditions so because of my STEM passion I want to become a medical journalist.

Have you ever been afraid to show people how smart you are in your chosen STEM field? If so, how do you deal with that?

I don't think I have ever been afraid to show off my skills in using technology or my fascination with medical struggles. Being in a Digital Design and Media Production class I used different software and I was also a yearbook class where we were responsible for using a program called Yearbook Avenue; technology was a must-have item that we all used to get the work done. I always excelled in getting the jobs done quickly and efficiently in all programs and it was something that always was fun for me to complete.

When did you first realize that you liked your STEM subject?

Ever since my sophomore year in high school, that's when I realized I had a passion for using technology to design various projects like informational brochures, advertisements, menus, and interactive videos. The Digital Design and Media Production class I took was a class that came naturally for me because I was responsible for having to know the skills for the various computer programs I had to use, as well as, having the use my creativity to generate all the unique assignments. That is when I decided I could use the computer and my writing skills to write a book to help other children see things differently about cleft-lip & palate challenges.

What would you tell another young lady who is coming to grips with her passion for STEM but afraid to fully embrace it?

I would tell her that she shouldn't be afraid to go for the subject that she knows the most. If she is good at math, science, technology, or engineering she should embrace it and use that talent to pursue a career in it. If she is afraid to pursue her passion for a subject, she should take additional classes that can help build her confidence and further ease her into becoming more successful with her passion. She should take advantage of school tutorials or get a job in a related field. Nobody should quit pursuing a dream just because it gets a bit tough at times. If she suffers a setback or even a failure, she should remember, she can always try it again! The possibilities are numerous and the paths are rewarding. She needs to reach for her dreams and take advantage of all the opportunities available to create the career she wants to have. Finally, she should not be afraid to try new things.

I think the biggest influence in a girl's life is having a "mentor" that they look up to and want to emulate. For example, I believe that a girl would be more likely to enter the STEM field if she has parent, relative, friend or teacher who has a career or an interest in STEM fields. Girl Scouts has been beneficial to many girls because in addition to exposure to STEM classes at school, the girls have the added benefit of taking advantage of the STEM opportunities within Girl Scouts. The girls are introduced to possible "mentors" through the various programs. The additional exposure enhances the possibility that a spark may be ignited for a STEM career. If a girl doesn't have a "mentor", she should look for one. She should take an inventory of the things that she excels in and realize that her career will be easier when her career choice matches her aptitude. She should embrace her abilities and not be afraid to shine. She should notice her peers and teachers being successful because that is how "mentors" are born.

Who is your biggest STEM influence and why?

My "mentor" is my dad. I've always looked up to my dad because ever since he was in elementary school, he was good in math. Even though he grew up in an environment where it wasn't as easy for him to get a higher education, he managed to take classes and earn a Master's degree in Electrical Engineering. He is successful because he is still excellent in math and has a love for new technology and he used these passions to excel as an Electrical Engineer.

What would you like to see more of in the STEM field?

Personally, I am satisfied with all the work that STEM has put into its program to help give certain girls a passion for what their good at in those subjects. However, I wish there would also be certain subjects like writing or reading that could also be combined with the other fields that take place. From past experience math and science aren't my strongest subjects but I still enjoy learning about technology and medical conditions.

Do you ever feel challenged in your STEM area that you have chosen?

At times, I do feel challenged in the field of technology because technology changes rapidly. It is constantly upgraded and new devices are always being developed, which means people must stay attentive to all that is happening to stay current. I must be prepared to adapt to change quickly and at times this is difficult to accomplish. However, technology upgrades provide brand new items that are to be utilized to help better the world.

Is there anything that you would change at your school that you believe would encourage more girls into the area of STEM?

I don't think there would be anything I would want to change regarding the issue of wanting to encourage more girls to take classes relating to math, science, technology, or engineering because there are many classes that cover those subjects. It's up to the girls' interests and passions on whether or not they want to take those classes and there's nothing more we could do to attract more people because there is already a good variety of classes and clubs that take place. Plano High Schools have many different classes that are offered for students in most subjects. They even have a special high school for STEM fields called the Academy High School. The school serves students from grades 9-12 and uses a STEAM educational approach for learning Science, Technology, Engineering, Arts and Math. I don't know if attending the Academy would have been better for me. I wish I had received more information about it. I assumed that is was just for students that wanted to go specifically into the medical field, engineering, math, science... I would encourage a girl to give a counselor a thorough list of her dreams, strengths and weaknesses and ask the counselor to go through all the available options with her before leaving middle school.

I don't know if all high schools provide the types of programs and courses that Plano schools provide, but if not, the programs should be created in those schools. Also, these programs should be encouraged in middle school too.

Do you often feel that you have to "prove yourself?" (i.e. do you feel that people do not respect your intelligence)?

I never feel as if I must prove myself because people who know that I am capable of anything I set my mind to, surround me. My school contains many students who are all good at unique things and everyone has a chance to show off their specific skills. There is no discrimination present, though there is competitiveness that takes place. But the competition served to motivate me to do my best and work hard to try and earn good grades and make a good future for myself.

AUDREY GUTGSELL

She is currently a student at Plano Senior High School in Texas and plans to pursue a career in Medical Journalism. Audrey Gutgsell decided to write "Open Smiles", a children's book about a girl's journey through the years as she was endured the ongoing surgeries and treatments to repair her cleft lip and palate. Audrey has published her book and has it available for free in a digital format, which has been included on several surgeons' websites throughout the country.

Challenges are what make life interesting and overcoming them is what makes life meaningful.

Joshua J. Marine

ADRIENNE HORTON

Why do you like the STEM field(s) that you like?

I love the engineering field because it requires you to use your mind. You would think I would like make up and dolls but I am not your average girl. I am different. I really like engineering because I love to build things. I love play-doh, Legos and sand because you can mold it into a lot of different things. I also love math because anything that has to do with numbers is right up my alley!

Taking this STEM passion, what do you envision yourself becoming (i.e. your ultimate career goal)?

My life goal is to be an engineer but I am not sure what field of engineering I would like to enter. I love to build and create things so I think this will be the best field for me.

Have you ever been afraid to show people how smart you are in your chosen STEM field? If so, how do you deal with that?

I have never been afraid to show how smart I am in my chosen STEM field. My mom always taught me to be proud of who I am so I have always done that. I think being smart is a gift!

When did you first realize that you liked your STEM subject?

I started to like engineering when I was just a baby by building my first Lego set. My mom said I would sit and build things for hours and I still do to this day. I learned to love math when I was in first grade. I had a great teacher and math always made me think so I fell in love with it.

What would you tell another young lady who is coming to grips with her passion for STEM but afraid to fully embrace it?

I would say there is nothing that can stop you but you. Don't be afraid to go for your dreams. If someone judges you let them know it does not change who you are. Embrace your talent no matter what the world says.

Who is your biggest STEM influence and why?

My biggest STEM influence is my dad, Nicholas Horton. He was an architect. He died when I was just a baby at the age of 29. My mom has told me a lot about him and his passion for STEM. He didn't get to fully live out his dream so I am excited to continue it for him. When talking about STEM fields my mom told me about engineering and I think it is the best fit for me.

What would you like to see more of in the STEM field?

I would love to see more girls in the STEM field. I hear a lot of girls talking about being singers and dancers but the world needs more female architects, engineers and scientists. I hope the STEM field has more programs to show girls how great this field is and how much they could help the world by joining this field.

Do you ever feel challenged in your STEM area that you have chosen?

Definitely! Math is one of the fields in STEM I am most interested in. When I learn something new like fractions it seems very hard at first but once I learn the concept it is so simple to me! I love the challenge and then discovering how easy it is.

Is there anything that you would change at your school that you believe would help encourage more girls into the area of STEM?

I would change things like letting girls bring make up and jewelry to school. That is why they are not paying attention in class. They are distracted by these things and not really embracing all that the STEM field has to offer.

Do you often feel that you have to "prove yourself "? I.e. do you feel that people do not respect your intelligence?

I don't feel like I have to prove myself. They accept that I am smart in the STEM field and often come to me when they need help with questions that they get wrong. I simply explain the questions to them and most times they understand and do better.

Name the last STEM project that you worked on that you were genuinely excited about? Why?

The last project I worked on was a science project on Gummy Bear Osmosis. It was awesome! The project required that you put gummy bears in different solutions to see how the gummy bear would react. It was interesting to see which liquids caused which reactions. It was crazy to think how different household items that we see every day could cause such different effects. I can't wait until my next science project!

ADRIENNE HORTON

My name is Adrienne Horton. I'm a shy, smart and studious individual. I think of myself as a serious person, although I've also been known to crack jokes whenever anyone needs a laugh. The things I love most in life are reading, watching cooking shows and Legos.

Limitations live only in our minds. But if we use our imaginations, our possibilities become limitless.

Jamie Paolinetti

JORDAN MANN

Why do you like the STEM field(s) that you like?

I've always had this weird fascination about science. I always liked to learn more about the matter around me and how certain things operate in the world. I've also been very curious about how it applies to me and how it affects the influence in medical science.

Taking this STEM passion, what do you envision yourself becoming (i.e. your ultimate career goal)?

My ideal career is to become a cardiologist. It's always been an interest of mine to work in the medical field and explore the cardiovascular system. I anticipate being heavily involved in research and eradicating heart disease in my community. I also see myself as an educator and helping people live a more healthy and productive lifestyle.

Have you ever been afraid to show people how smart you are in your chosen STEM field? If so, how do you deal with that?

I'm never afraid to show off my intelligence. It just shows people that whatever they do I can do 10x better. My intelligence is a part of who I am and I will never fear showing people a part of me. I don't see being intelligent and focused as a fear. I see my characteristics as a strength and hopefully those around me are inspired in some way.

When did you first realize that you liked your STEM subject?

Early in my education, I recognized that I gravitated towards an interest in science more than any other subject. Now that I'm in high school, science plays a more prevalent role for me. It has expanded my thinking, increased my curiosity and made me even more interested. I'm excited about the possibilities and potential that my future interest will garner.

What would you tell another young lady who is coming to grips with her passion for STEM but afraid to fully embrace it?

I would tell her to not be afraid to cherish the inner brightness in her. If any female can do it, she can most definitely can do it herself. I would also tell her to turn that passion into more than just a dream, but into something tangible that could change the world.

Who is your biggest STEM influence and why?

I don't have a STEM influence per se, however after viewing and reading about Hidden Figures and those remarkable black women, I was even more inspired. To know that history and a foundation existed, I'm even more excited to follow in the footsteps of courageous and inspirational women such as Ms. Vaughn, Ms. Johnson and Ms. Jackson. I hope that I'm able to have a legacy such as theirs as well as create my own foundation for others to be inspired as well.

What would you like to see more of in the STEM field?

I would like to see more details about human anatomy and physiology rather than how it works and what it does. I would like to be exposed in the classroom and in everyday life to opportunities that will give young women such as myself a deeper understanding of the various aspects of STEM (Science, Technology, Engineering and Math). They all play a vital role in our world and it would be great to have more exposure in all fields.

Do you ever feel challenged in your STEM area that you have chosen?

I've never felt challenged in my STEM field. I enjoy being able to overthink and rationalize how things are in a scientific setting.

Is there anything that you would change at your school that you believe would help encourage more girls into the area of STEM?

I would get the teachers and administrators to engage us more about STEM and allow girls to build their confidence. At my school, it's usually hard to get people interested in just basic subjects. To get them interested in STEM subjects our administration would have to show students the value and long term benefits that STEM adds in our world.

Do you often feel that you must "prove yourself "? I.e. do you feel that people do not respect your intelligence?

Absolutely not! I'm well respected by my peers and I don't down play my intelligence for no one. I'm confident and when people think of Jordan Mann they automatically know that I exude and present intelligence in everything I do. I'm respected by my teachers, family and friends because of my overwhelming dedication to my goals.

Name the last STEM project that you worked on that you were genuinely excited about? Why?

My last STEM project involved the study of mitosis and demonstrating the cycles. I learned how cancer was caused by nonstop mitosis and I was fascinated at the origin of cancer. I was immediately struck by the fact that something such as cancer has blanketed society. To see the many cycles of mitosis and how cancerous cells are created, I was highly involved in the project. I created a poster board that chronicled the many cycles and how each one evolved. I used different material found in my home to outline the sequence of cycles. It was a fun experience and my teacher and classmates were very motivated to hear more about it. I enjoyed the time, effort and research I put in the project.

JORDAN MANN

Jordan has always made it a point to strive for her goals. She attends Red Oak High school where she consistently excels academically. In her spare time, Jordan enjoys spending time with her family, playing soccer, and volunteering. Jordan would like to attend LSU and major in Biology. She would also like to further her college studies by attending medical school in pursuit of a career in cardiology.

You become what you believe.
Oprah Winfrey

KAIBA AUTUMN MURPHY

Why do you like the STEM field(s) that you like?

Math challenges me to look for the possibilities and limitations in everything.

Taking this STEM passion, what do you envision yourself becoming (i.e. your ultimate career goal)?

Being an engineer is my ultimate career goal. Right now, I am exploring the various types of engineering. I'm currently attending workshops focused on aeronautical and mechanical engineering.

Have you ever been afraid to show people how smart you are in your chosen STEM field? If so, how do you deal with that?

There are times during math class, when I try and moderate my mathematical aptitude as I maybe exceeding my classmate's level of understanding. During those times, I ask the teacher to review my work, hoping it demonstrates that I need assistance and that it's okay to seek help if needed.

When did you first realize that you liked your STEM subject?

I realized my passion for math in the fourth grade. The lessons were exciting and I wanted to learn more! A lesson that really ignited my passion for math was learning how equations are used to resolve everyday activities. It spiked my love for math because I never looked at the stop light, train signals or my tablet the same way.

What would you tell another young lady who is coming to grips with her passion for STEM but afraid to fully embrace it?

Don't be afraid to embrace your passions, you should always try and live up to your own potential. You never know how far it can take you.

Who is your biggest STEM influence and why?

As a native Texan, from the Dallas area, my influences are all around me, from my math teachers, to the engineers that I have met through my mother's sorority and college. I interact daily with women who exhibit their passion for math and science. They proudly mentor and encourage me.

What would you like to see more of in the STEM field?

More females in powerful, influential positions in the STEM field.

Do you ever feel challenged in your STEM area that you have chosen?

Yes, I do feel challenged when learning a new mathematical concept, which leads to a high sense of satisfaction once I master the concept.

Is there anything that you would change at your school that you believe would help encourage more girls into the area of STEM?

Having more hands on and team experiences, like a hack a thon. This would be a great ice breaker into the field.

Do you often feel that you have to "prove yourself "? I.e. do you feel that people do not respect your intelligence?

Although I think people do respect and appreciate my intelligence, I have experienced challenges to my responses. Once my response to an algebraic term was challenged by a few male classmates, I referred and shared a lesson learned during my Summer TexPrep Course to verify I was correct.

Name the last STEM project that you worked on that you were genuinely excited about?

During a recent aeronautical engineering workshop, we were tasked with building and testing our own plane. We had to calculate wind resistance to determine design and duration of flight. It was exciting to practice rapid iteration, via testing and re-working models based on calculations.

KAIBA AUTUMN MURPHY

"The good life is one inspired by love and guided by knowledge."
-Bertrand Russell

"Am I living up to my fullest potential?" is the question Autumn asks herself every day. Even at the age of fourteen she has strived to be her best in every way possible. Her career goal is to become an engineer. As for now, she is taking strides in making her career goals a reality. As an eighth-grade student attending Red Oak Middle School, she is a member of the National Junior Honor Society, Yearbook Staff, Tennis Team and a member of the UIL Mathematics Team. She is also a 3rd year student of the TexPrep Pre-Freshman Engineering Program. Understanding that a life well lived includes service to others, Autumn is a math tutor and a Cadet in the Girl Scouts of Northeast Texas. In her spare time, Autumn likes to participate in tennis tournaments with the USTA, play video games, build Lego communities, and spend time with family and friends.

I have learned over the years that when one's mind is made up, this diminishes fear.

Rosa Parks

CORDEJAH WALKER

Why do you like the STEM field(s) that you like?

I have an intense passion for engineering. I feel this field possess the most creative people among the four. It is responsible for creating and designing what we use every day. Engineers help construct our world. We solve problems to question and create new items that you never knew you wanted. I have a different outlook on the world and create products that improve it either on a local or global scale. I can help people across the world by creating solutions to problems that are crippling nations.

Engineering incorporates many different fields. The main ones are math, science and technology. However, inspiration for solutions can come from anywhere. Many designs are influenced by art, history and human nature. The multiple inspirations allow for collaboration with not only people in your field, but also people in very different fields as well. Working together, with intellect and creativity allows for innovative and innovative ideas to become reality. I love the wonderful feeling of accomplishment when you create something that helps or caters to a need. The satisfaction from this field is unlike no other which led me to loving this field.

Taking this STEM passion, what do you envision yourself becoming (i.e. your ultimate career goal)?

My career aspirations are to become a mechanical engineer and work on projects that help further our understanding in a particular subject. Examples of companies who are doing this is NASA and Tesla Inc. These companies and many others are constantly working to increase our knowledge in various subjects. I feel as though I would thrive in this type of work and want to be a valuable asset and contributor.

Have you ever been afraid to show people how smart you are in your chosen STEM field? If so, how do you deal with that?

During my academic career, there have times where I have restrained from voicing my opinion or stating the correct answer in fear people would become upset. I dreaded being called the know-it-all. So many times, I said nothing, which later would cause problems because the solution or project was wrong. The older I became I realized that if I can contribute to a situation positively, then I should say what I need to say. I carried this ideology in my chosen STEM field of technology. In my engineering classes, most students are male. At first I was intimidated by them, but the more I begun to have correct answers or better designs, the more I felt confident and could voice my intellect.

Never be afraid to show your intellect! Even if you feel people feel you know too much, do not let that hold you back. I have come up with a method. If you know the answer or solution right away, allow other students a chance to answer. If no one can answer correctly, then give your answer. This allows for people to gain their education and allows for you to help them out in a nice way. Once you show your intelligence, more people will ask for help, and you will be able to positively contribute to you class. Do not be afraid to be yourself and show your knowledge. You will positively contribute to the people you are around by sharing it.

When did you first realize that you liked your STEM subject?

On my eleventh birthday, I was given a toy robot that double as a penny bank. The robot moved around and spoke encouraging words each time you placed a coin into it. I was so amazed and began to wonder about how it worked. I looked up the robot on the internet and saw the different versions and improvements people had created. I tried to emulate their creation for my own robot. I checked out books from the local library about robotics and engineering trying to understand what they had done.

I asked my mother for certain supplies but she did not have any clue what they were. I resorted to taking apart unwanted devices to get the supplies I needed. I began to work on the robot. The first modification was to extend the arms so that I could reach objects I could not. The second was to have to the robot be remote controlled. I also wanted the robot to do math problem since it already could display numbers. I essentially wanted a robot butler that could do my homework.

I worked on it every day after school for about a month. My efforts were very ambitious and consequently, it did not do what I wanted. Afterwards, I became infatuated with robots and engineering. I began to work on and come up with my own inventions. As grew up, I kept my love for creation and inventing and took classes on robotics and engineering. I now desire to major in mechanical engineering in college. One little robot began a new path for my life.

What would you tell another young lady who is coming to grips with her passion for STEM but afraid to fully embrace it?

Deciding to be in STEM is one of the best decisions you will make. If you enjoy making things, doing math, creating science experiments, working on a computer, or anything that challenges you, STEM is for you. You will be able to create and discover things that you cannot in other fields. There are so many different things you can do that combines your passions with STEM. Let's say you like to draw but you also like cars. You could create a car based on your drawing. You can combine anything you do with STEM. There are so many various aspects of these fields that allows you to incorporate STEM while also doing other things you love. The possibilities are endless in these fields. The only thing holding you back is your imagination. So, give STEM a try, you will not regret it.

Who is your biggest STEM influence and why?

My biggest STEM influence is my current engineering and robotics teacher (one person teaches both). Her name is Ms. Petty. She is an electrical engineer and is the only African-American woman that I have personal known that is an engineer. She has seen and recommended me to so many opportunities in engineering and that has helped me grow not only as a person, but has placed me much closer to becoming an engineer. She is also encouraging me to do more and participate in activities that she knows are perfect for me. Along with assignments she gives me in class, she allows me time to work on other opportunities and helps in any way she can.

She is a prime example that African- American women such as myself can become engineers.

What would you like to see more of in the STEM field?

The one aspect I feel STEM fields lacks are women. There are not nearly enough women in STEM. A study done in 2012 shows that women make up less than 30% of STEM jobs. Of this 30%, only 8% of them are mechanical engineers. Women are extremely underrepresented in STEM. There are so many jobs available, and STEM fields would only improve with the inclusion of more women.

Another aspect I feel STEM lacks along with women is diversity. A study done in 2016 show that about 70% of STEM jobs are done by Caucasian people in America. Leaving only 30% of jobs held by minorities. Of those monitories women are a very scarce. Minority women make up one out of ten of those jobs. We need more women and minorities in STEM. STEM does not just affect one group of people. We need more representation of the other groups. The more people with diverse backgrounds allows for different perspectives and ways for solving problems. This will in turn help everyone not just that one group. There needs to be more diversity in STEM.

Do you ever feel challenged in your STEM area that you have chosen?

All the time, but that is what I love about engineering. I enjoy thinking about innovative solutions to problems or coming up with an entirely new idea. I am constantly looking around trying to see what I can improve or what could be done differently. I try to write down any idea that comes to mind. Many times, I will come up with an idea that is completely crazy, but still write it down. Even though the idea may seem absurd, combined with other ideas it can create something that is amazing. If you think about it, a century ago much of the technology we have today seemed completely crazy and would have not been taken seriously. Just think about a few decades ago, the modern computer was just being developed. Now computers are a part of our daily lives. Do you know that a phone today is better and faster than what was used to guide man to the moon! That trip was a challenge back then and they succeeded.

Challenges create inspiration for creation. I always want to be challenged to be better or do better. You will not grow if you are never challenged. Think about a child learning to walk. Someone held them up by their hands and guided them to walk. They stumbled and fell many times, but eventually began to walk on their own. At that time, it was a challenge but it allowed them to grow as a person. I keep this mindset in engineering. At first it was very difficult, I felt as though I was three steps behind everything my teacher taught. Eventually, with hard work I caught up and did extremely well in class. Now I have the luxury of being able to understand quickly and help others on projects. You need challenges in whatever you do. Just think about it, would you want to do the same thing repeatedly? No, and engineering allows for me to be challenged and helps me grow not only as an engineer but as a person.

Is there anything that you would change at your school that you believe would help encourage more girls into the area of STEM?

My school has many classes in STEM. Many students including myself will graduate with an endorsement in whatever elective classes we took for four years. They are very informative and allows us to learn more about a career. We also can be an intern while at school. I really enjoy my endorsement engineering classes and many others do as well.

The problem is, in my engineering class there are not many girls. This applies to every STEM endorsement class at my school. Girls usually choose endorsements in the arts or language areas. If I could change anything at my school it would be to create a class where freshman students are exposed to every endorsement. It would consist of the students participating in different fields of study. That way more girls would be exposed to STEM, which could cause more girls to become interested and involved in STEM. I would also create a STEM club especially for girls. We could learn more about STEM and compete in competitions. I believe that many girls are not in STEM because they do not see their peers or other women in STEM. If they are exposed and see more girls and women in STEM, then more will become interested and involved.

Do you often feel that you have to "prove yourself "? I.e. do you feel that people do not respect your intelligence?

I do not feel I must prove myself as often I did when started engineering. When I began my first engineering class in the ninth grade, I was very intimidated by my classmates. Many were upperclassmen and very intelligent. In my first project, I was placed in a group of four. I was the only girl and freshman in the group. When brainstorming ideas, I would try to voice my ideas but it would be drowned out by the other guys talking. The idea they came up with was not compliant with the rubric guidelines and would result in a low grade. I explained the problem with the idea but they ignored me and did it anyway. I decided to do my own project. They turned in their project and got a falling grade. I turned in my project and received the highest grade.

Once everyone knew my grade, I gained respect from the class and could work well in groups. That experience taught me to that I needed to convey my ideas and opinions more effectively. Now I do not have to prove my intelligence as often as before.

Name the last STEM project that you worked on that you were genuinely excited about? Why?

Myself and three other girls attended a workshop for girls in STEM. It consisted of women from major STEM companies, businesses, and colleges to talk to us about the possibilities in STEM. A day before we were given a challenge to make a floatable drone that could collect water samples for a competition. We were supposed to have the material to build it weeks before but were notified about the work shop late and only had one day to build.

The drone had a Styrofoam base and additional mechanical parts. Attached to the Styrofoam was a crane connected to a plastic cup that could be controlled by a remote. The cup is lowered into the water to collect it. To make the drone move in water, I created two propellers that was also controlled by the remote. The whole built took about three hours with dedicated work from the four of us.

When we arrived at the workshop, we placed the drone in a pool of water. To win, our drone had to successfully complete a trip around the pool, stop in a designated place, and collect a water sample. We did our turn and it was a success. We won the competition. This was the first time I had worked with a drone, let alone a drone in water. I enjoy the rush of trying to complete the drone in such a short amount of time and would love to do something like that again.

CORDEJAH WALKER

Cordejah Walker was born in Indiana and now resides in Texas since age 15. A junior in high school, she participates in engineering and robotic courses. She aspires to become a mechanical engineer. She is a NASA High School Aerospace Scholar, and was accepted into the MITES program at MIT.

Follow effective actions with quiet reflection. From the quiet reflection will come even more effective action."

Peter Drucker

About AMS Academic Solutions

AMS Academic Solutions is a subsidiary under Alexis M Services LLC. Alexis M Services LLC is a certified MBE (Minority Business Enterprise) and a certified HUB (Historically Underutilized Business) in the state of Texas. This company is owned and operated by Alexis M. Scott.

AMS Academic Solutions provides one-on-one and group tutoring to students in the convenience of their home or somewhere near their residence at a time convenient to them. AMS Academic Solutions also gives the student the option of in person tutoring or instruction via an online whiteboard.

53311674R00065

Made in the USA
San Bernardino, CA
13 September 2017